Memories of Yellow Tears

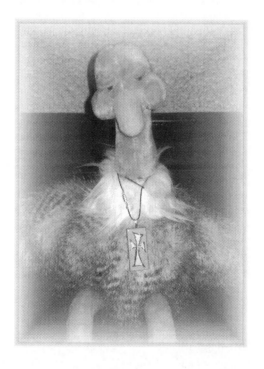

Phillis Knox

WESTBOW
PRESS
A DIVISION OF THOMAS NELSON

WestBow Press books may be ordered through booksellers or by contacting:

WestBow Press
A Division of Thomas Nelson
1663 Liberty Drive
Bloomington, IN 47403
www.westbowpress.com
1-(866) 928-1240

ISBN: 978-1-4497-8098-2 (sc)
ISBN: 978-1-4497-8097-5 (e)

Library of Congress Control Number: 2012924259

Printed in the United States of America

WestBow Press rev. date: 2/01/2013

To Robbie and Kay Jones,
a big thank-you for remembering me with the
gift of life.
And to Carolyn Mitchell and Fay Moore
for their assistance in making this book happen.

Contents

Prologue ix

Chapter 1   Lurking Within 1

Chapter 2   Ouch! 5

Chapter 3   Horrors: The "C" Word 11

Chapter 4   I Passed! 17

Chapter 5   A Shade of Orange 23

Chapter 6   Vascular Data 29

Chapter 7   Us Four and No More! 35

Chapter 8   Job Well Done 39

Chapter 9   Unexpected Call 45

Chapter 10 Ready! Set! Go! 49

Chapter 11 The Grand Finale 53

Epilogue 59

The Ultimate Gift 61

Prologue

The year that I turned forty was a major turning point in my life. My husband and I had another child. Little did I know, however, that my life was like a spark that would soon explode into a blazing fire.

My liver was deteriorating from a disease that I was unfamiliar with (primary biliary cirrhosis). I learned that this particular disease had many phases that one must go through, and as much as I dreaded the thought, I had to go through this illness alone. I was afraid, plain and simple. There was no doubt that this disease could and would eventually kill me.

I faced a long, fearsome journey. I had never before realized that God was right there walking with me every step of the way. This is a story about my thoughts, family, fears, medical tests, and the transplant itself, a process that spanned five months of my life during which I remained in the end stage of a severe liver disease. It was during this time that I really came to know the Lord in a way I had never known Him before. My strength came from Him with the support of my family and friends.

In my book, you will see how powerful prayer is and how much more affecting it can be when offered up by larger numbers of people. It took me a long time to realize that my illness may have actually been a blessing. Had I not been sick, I may never have come to know the Lord like I did (and do now). One thing's for sure: my life was spared for a reason, and I will be forever grateful.

CHAPTER I

Lurking Within

While I was sitting at home and gazing out the window, I asked myself if most people realized how fortunate they were just to be alive. I certainly did. The past fifteen years of my life had definitely been a challenge, but when I thought of the past twelve months, waves of mixed emotions and memories washed over me in thanksgiving.

It all began with my annual physical in 1993. I never dreamed that anything was wrong. I felt really good. In fact, I had returned to school, given birth to my third child (when I was forty years old), raised two grown sons, and enjoyed a wonderful husband. Then ... boom! The phone rang, and the message on the other end held anything but good news. My liver enzymes were extremely elevated, and a biopsy would be needed. I could not help but wonder what all that meant. I thought maybe there had been a mistake, but there wasn't.

A few weeks later, a doctor performed a biopsy. I had primary biliary cirrhosis. I had no idea what that was; however, I knew it had to be bad, and indeed it was. I was scared! In time, this disease killed its victims.

There I was, with a five-year-old little girl. She was a "change-of-life baby," and oh, what we had gone through to keep from losing her prior to the delivery date. That was a horrible pregnancy, and it had resulted in three months of frequent hospital stays. She may have been unplanned, but she was no accident. God is good and blessed us with a healthy, beautiful little girl.

Many thoughts went through my mind after I received the alarming diagnosis about my liver disease. What would happen to my young child? I wanted so much to be the one to raise her.

Time steadily moved on, and my health remained pretty good. I was on one particular medication that had seemingly slowed the progression of the disease. Nevertheless, I wasn't about to take life for granted, and I found myself praying more than ever before.

When Jackie started school, I went to work in the public school system, substituting in both elementary and high school classes. That kept me busy for the next eight years. Work not only enabled me to share school days with Jackie but also kept my mind occupied, shifting the focus off my health issues.

Other than the usual blood work required because of the disease, there were no other major health problems. I sometimes wondered if it were possible that the disease had vanished altogether. That was wishful thinking. I knew the answer to that unspoken question. The disease was like a cancer and had only gone into remission.

As much as possible, my husband and I tried to live a fairly normal life—if you can call raising a teenager in your fifties "normal." The challenge certainly kept us on our toes! Our two sons, Scottie and Jody, were already married with families of their own. The whole family (right down to aunts, uncles, and cousins) was close, and I knew that bond would be important in the days ahead. We all prayed for one another, and that is what I wanted and needed most—prayer.

There was never a day that went by when I didn't think about the awful disease lurking within my body. I knew that it would be good to share my thoughts with someone, but that was something that I found very difficult to do, even with my own family. Maybe I thought that if I talked about the sickness, if I said something about how it affect me aloud, then that would validate it or make it more real than I was willing or ready to accept.

After the initial diagnosis, thirteen years passed with no major problems, but then things began to slowly change. My blood work revealed that my enzymes and bilirubin were more elevated. It was then that I realized the disease was steadily getting worse—not drastically bad but worse. I had often hoped that things would improve if I got more exercise and concentrated on a better diet, but there was no change.

Jaundice began to set in. My skin took on a yellowish tint, and my eyes looked muddy. People began to notice, and I could see the fear in their eyes when they looked at me. They knew that my liver was getting worse.

Not only was my skin color changing, but my legs and feet were beginning to swell. They were so tight at times that I thought they would actually burst. Naturally, I tried to justify this change by saying I had been on my feet more than usual.

It was so hard to believe that I was getting worse, but I was. I was yellow, with swollen legs and feet and an eczema-like rash on both legs. This, too, had become a real problem. My legs looked like they had suffered second-degree burns most of the time, like some accident victim's legs whose dark bruises had turned bluish yellow. Finally, I found prescription lotions as well as over-the-counter medications that helped. While taking these treatments and sitting in the sun didn't cure the rashes, they did help tremendously.

I knew that there was no need for me to really complain. After all, God had blessed me, and I knew it. He had allowed me to raise my daughter. That is what I had asked for, so how could I possibly ask for more? The Lord not only allowed me to raise her but to see her married. What a beautiful wedding it was. It was such a special occasion, and I knew that Charlie, our new son-in-law, would love and take excellent care of her. They did make a beautiful couple, and we were all pleased.

Following the wedding, however, a drastic change took place, and I found myself getting extremely tired each day. All the festivities had taken their toll, and about six months later, severe problems with my health evolved. It was the beginning of a long, tedious journey.

*Thought for today:*_____

"Don't worry about anything; instead pray about everything. Tell God what you need, and thank him for all he has done" (Philippians 4:6 NLT).

CHAPTER 2

Ouch!

"Hello, January," I said to myself. The year 2009 sauntered in, presenting a noticeable contrast to the recently festive holiday activities. I had barely finished storing the tree decorations when I came down with an unusual virus. My fever was extremely high; however, there were no other symptoms. Nevertheless, the holidays were over, and all who came to visit, both friends and family, had returned to their homes. People are often left with feelings of melancholy following busy, enjoyable holidays, and this postseason time felt that way to me.

Sometimes we get so caught up in today's demanding lifestyle and personal obligations that we fail to notice the simple pleasures of the good old days until something happens to jolt those memories. I fully realized these as if some deep, gnawing awareness lurked just below my level of consciousness. For days, I sat and reminisced about the wonderful holidays that my sister, Jeanie, and I once enjoyed as young children. I visualized Dad packing the car with all the Christmas gifts before we headed to Grandma's house in

Eustis, Florida. There, we opened our gifts from Santa and enjoyed a huge turkey dinner with other family members. I relished the wonderful memories filled with so much excitement and love.

It all began with my daily bath. While I was relaxing in the tub, a severe cramp suddenly grasped me on my upper right side under my ribcage. My only thought was this: *Please, God, help me. I can't move.* I had had body cramps in the past, but never anything like this and never in that particular area. Any kind of muscle strain or pull that had previously occurred was mostly confined to my legs or feet. Nearly an hour after the paralyzing pain struck, I was finally able to stand and get out of the tub. The whole experience left me sore and with a persistent feeling that something was lodged between my ribs.

Although I knew that I should share my painful experience with my husband, Murray, I hesitated because I didn't want to alarm him. I did tell him, though, and after a long discussion, we decided a good night's sleep might be the best remedy. On almost every occasion and on every issue, Murray was much more optimistic than I was. My attitude was usually gloom and doom, and in this case, it was definitely just that—more gloom and doom.

The following afternoon, I didn't feel any better. I felt a constant heaviness on that side, as if a weight was pressing on my upper abdomen. I realized it was time to get another opinion, and the first person who popped into my mind was Jeanie, a registered nurse.

Jeanie and I had always had a close relationship, so it was only natural for me to reach out to her. Jeanie and her husband, Johnny, were still nearby at their home in Alabama, but I knew they would soon be Montana-bound to spend the spring and summer months in Glacier Park.

I contacted Jeanie and explained every detail of my episode in the tub. She thought that I might have a gallstone. If I were having gall bladder problems, I would need a change in diet—one omitting fried, greasy foods. I made some adjustments to my daily menu, but I noticed little or no improvement.

Another week passed, and there was still no change, so Jeanie suggested that I see one of the doctors at Community Hospital in Tallassee, Alabama, where she had been employed for many years. That was fine with me. I was getting desperate for some relief. I scheduled an appointment with Dr. Tom Bianchi, a well-known and highly respected gastroenterologist. Dr. Bianchi had previously treated me for colitis and was familiar with my liver condition.

During my visit with Dr. Bianchi, he suggested several tests, beginning with an endoscopy followed by a colonoscopy. Toward the end of the week, I was prepped for the procedures and had both tests done. I was so shocked to learn the test results indicated no evidence of gallstones, only a little sludge, but excessive inflammation in the abdomen. Next, he prescribed strong antibiotics to clear up the inflammation, so we all thought the malady would soon end.

Another week passed, and there was still no improvement, so I called Dr. Bianchi again. He suggested I go into the hospital and receive the antibiotic intravenously to allow the medication to enter my system much faster and more efficiently. Shortly thereafter, I was admitted to the hospital, and a nurse administered the IV along with additional tests that needed to be conducted. The battery of tests began with blood work, an ultrasound, and a CT scan. My veins were starting to collapse from being pricked so many times. It seemed as if every procedure brought some new challenge, and it was at that time when I started wondering if all the complications could be associated with my liver disorder.

Later that evening, I learned that Dr. Bianchi had contacted Dr. Steve Bynon, one of the three liver transplant surgeons at UAB, the University of Alabama Hospital at Birmingham. Both doctors agreed it would be necessary for me to transfer immediately to UAB, where they could perform more extensive testing. They ruled out the gall bladder, and so the reality of my possible condition was finally beginning to sink in. The events of the day only strengthened my fears of a serious liver ailment.

What a surprise! While we were waiting to be discharged, who should walk in but our son, Jody, who lives in Birmingham? Bless his heart, he had come to check on me, and after he had heard all the details about me being transferred, he insisted on taking us himself. That was fine with me because the hospital had arranged to send me by ambulance, which had always been one of my phobias. We were not sure that Dr. Bianchi would approve the move, but reluctantly, he did. Within an hour, the call came that UAB had a room waiting for me.

It is certainly true what they say about love and kindness always shining through because I personally experienced these from the fantastic nursing staff at Tallassee Hospital. Such thoughts raced through my mind as we departed and headed north. Around ten o'clock, we reached UAB. Deep in my soul, I knew the short journey to Birmingham had ended but that my long journey had just begun.

*Thought for today:*_____

"Be strong and courageous. Do not fear or be in dread of them, for it is the Lord your God who goes with you. He will not leave you or forsake you" (Deuteronomy 31:6 TLB).

CHAPTER 3

Horrors: The "C" Word

Wow! UAB was like a city within itself. It was so good that Jody was able to bring us. He knew just exactly where to go and what to do, which was a blessing to us. After admission, we were taken to the eighth floor, which was located in the Spain Wallace Center, where the nurses were awaiting my arrival. I was in a strange place now. I didn't know a soul, and I was scared to death. However, to my surprise, the room appointed to me had two beds.

I had hoped for a private room but was thrilled when I learned that Murray could use the other bed, which meant so much to me. My fears were so many, and only he knew and understood them all. Shortly after I settled in, the nurse informed us that the doctor would not be in until morning. That was fine with us because we were both exhausted and ready for bed.

Little did we know that the early morning hours would consist of a CAT scan followed by blood work. By "early," I mean 3:00 a.m., so sleep would not be an important factor during this hospital stay. This scan was supposed to be more precise than the previous

11

ones. Upon completion, I was taken back to my room for possibly another hour of sleep. Murray was sleeping so soundly that I tried not to disturb him.

Later in the morning, family started coming to visit. What a wonderful surprise! After all, most of them lived at least two hours away. It wasn't like they were just around the corner. I appreciated all of them so much. Not only were they family, but they were the best prayer warriors one could have. Oh, how I needed prayer, and prayer is what I got. I learned that I had been added to many prayer lists in churches throughout the United States.

Everyone seemed to be there with the exception of my daughter, Jackie. She was pregnant with her first child and terribly sick with eclampsia. (We didn't know about the dangerous disease then, but we would soon learn.) Then Dr. Eckhoff, one of the three transplant surgeons, entered the room. He wanted to inform us that Dr. Bynon was out of town and would be back Monday morning. In the meantime, Dr. Eckhoff had studied some of my recent scans, and according to him, there was a good possibility that the lower end of the liver contained a cancerous tumor. He then presented a sketch drawing of the organ, and I must admit that my liver looked anything but normal. It was covered with nodules. In fact, it actually resembled a cluster of grapes.

Just the thought of a tumor was horrifying to me. What would happen now? Everything was happening so fast, but thank goodness others were there to help me understand.

We learned that a tumor in that particular location was often better than ones in other areas because there were no bone structures or major vessels around the liver; therefore, cancer in that area would be less likely to spread. Dr. Eckhoff went on to explain how a tumor could not exceed 5.0cm for a transplant. The guidelines had been set by the United Network for Organ Sharing. The tumor was about that size from what they could see. Dr. Eckhoff proceeded to tell us about the MELD score and how it was used with end-stage liver disease. For example, when I entered the hospital, my MELD score was around fifteen, but if the doctors indeed found a tumor, that discovery would raise my score to twenty-one or twenty-two. The MELD score gave a general idea of the severity of the disease. When someone is added to the transplant waiting list, the waiting period depends on the blood type, the severity of the person's illness, height, weight, and organ availability. I needed many more tests for evaluation to ensure that everything was working properly.

It was definitely going to be tough, but I was determined. I didn't understand everything very well, but I knew I wanted to live. God was there walking me through.

On the following day, some of the family, including our two sons, returned to meet with and hear what Dr. Bynon had to say. In fact, he walked in shortly after their arrival. Everything we discussed was similar to the information we had gotten from Dr. Eckhoff, the exception being his desire for another test to confirm that there was indeed a tumor. He wanted an MRI performed that morning. After I had spoken with both doctors, I knew that I was definitely in good hands. Both appeared to be very competent.

The MRI did not take too long, and almost as soon as I returned to the room, Dr. Bynon came back inside. He wanted to discuss our insurance. Apparently, the hospital's system had me listed with a former insurance company that we no longer used. Undoubtedly, the provider was one that UAB did not accept. However, the good news came quickly that we had the top-of-the-line insurance, which had been effective since the first of the year. Although the administration had failed to enter the current insurance information, a nurse came in to confirm that the data had been updated and that we did indeed have the preferred insurance coverage. I was glad to know this mix-up had been resolved. Had that not been the case, this story might have ended differently. Thank you, Lord! This was definitely a blessing.

It had been a long day, and the family members had all said their goodbyes. I really enjoyed each one of them. After everyone left, I found myself just living in a daze when I suddenly noticed a little critter sitting on my bedside table. My sister, Jeanie, had brought me an unusual stuffed animal to cheer me. It was an emu. The first thing that came to mind was how dorky it looked with its long legs, big feet, little head, and fat body with wings. That was certainly the right description—dorky! It turned out to be such a conversation piece that I named it Dorcas. It wasn't until later that I learned that Dorcas was someone mentioned in the Bible in Acts 9:39–42. Turns out that was a Greek name for Tabitha. She was a woman who did kind deeds and was brought back to life by Peter. Dorcas was given a second chance at life. I could not believe what I heard. It may have been a coincidence, but it sure happened at the right time. As I look back, I realize how I, too, was given a second chance at life. Thank you, Lord! Dorcas became my little mascot, and it still is to this day.

"Don't be afraid, for I am with you. Don't be discouraged, for I am your God. I will strengthen you and help you. I will hold you up with my victorious right hand" (Isaiah 41:10 NLT).

Dorcus (my little mascot)

15

CHAPTER 4

I Passed!

Talk about goosebumps. My skin was crawling with them as we entered the driveway. We were home, yet everything seemed different to me. I was no longer the energetic person I used to be. The liver disease, primary biliary cirrhosis, had taken its toll on my entire system. I worried about my situation and also Jackie's health. Just knowing that she and the baby were in grave danger was a constant worry, and we all knew our hands were tied.

It was early evening when we noticed some headlights turning outside. It was Jeanie and Johnny. They had come by to inquire about some tests from earlier that morning. What in the world would I do without those two? Johnny had been in the family since I had turned eleven years old, and he was more like a brother to me than a brother-in-law. And of course, Jeanie had been there since day one. Admittedly, both of them had really taught me a lot of things about life, especially about the *Bible*. Although reading had never been one of my favorite pastimes, they showed me how to study and apply the scriptures to my life today. I needed that.

Their daughter, Kaye, was another jewel that touched my heart during that time. She was our little songbird, and when she sang, she sounded like one of the angels in heaven. If she weren't singing to me, she was quoting scripture and then closing with a beautiful prayer. She was definitely an inspiration to me, and we love her dearly.

Another week ended, and it was time to return to UAB for more testing. We would stay once again with Jody and Becky. I loved being with our children because they would give me a lift when no one else could. I feel so sad when I think of all those who have no one in their lives. That thought reminds me of how we need to do more for others and how no one should ever to be alone.

On my appointment day, the car was packed and ready to leave. I knew the tests this time would be a little different because a psychiatric exam had been added, probably to make sure I was a stable person and not a little bit crazy.

I was in great pain by the day's end because the trip was so hard on me. Two hours in a car without stopping was pretty rough, especially with my side. I was not really good company for anyone, although Jessie, my ten-year-old granddaughter, managed to keep my mind occupied. Children at that age can really come up with some cute little problems of their own. Well, Jessie managed to keep my attention all evening. I guess that's why they are called *grand*children. All of mine, including Justin, Jennifer, Jessie, Brady, and Isabella, are just that—*grand!*

Early the next morning while it was still dark outside, we arrived at the hospital. The size of UAB always amazed me. It was a good thing we knew right where to go. During the first day,

I had several tests done on my heart that lasted a couple of hours. However, I was still dreading the psychiatric exam scheduled for after lunch. The tests crawled on for hours. I knew that all of this was terribly difficult on Murray, but he really never complained. I was so blessed to have such a wonderful, supportive husband.

Finally, lunchtime arrived, and we were able to enjoy a rather tasty meal and take a much needed break. The hospital cafeteria served great food, which is usually not the case in many medical facilities.

Following lunch, a doctor administered the psychiatric exams. We found the exam location, which was a considerable distance from the cafeteria; however, we managed to find it, and I signed myself in. Although I thought the exam would last two hours at max, it turned out to be a long afternoon. Boy I was so wrong! I honestly did not think I would ever finish, but I did. Because I didn't really know what the testing would include, I was surprised by many of the questions. For example, one section involved looking at diagrams that were complex and resembled structures found in a physical science textbook. There was nothing simple about the entire testing procedure. I was happy when it finally ended because I was exhausted and my side hurting something awful. The entire day had been quite an experience.

After I returned home, things seemed to settle down a little bit. I rested much of the time, and Murray returned to work. During that time period, his company made many adjustments and mentioned early retirement to several of their employees. Although Murray had not planned to retire for several more years, we both agreed it would be perfect timing. Of course, there would be many options to explore and many details to address. After he initiated the process, Murray's last day of employment with his company came to an end. The company planned a retirement dinner for a later date, but unfortunately, we missed the celebration because I was scheduled to be back in Birmingham. We were both so disappointed, but we knew God's plan was the best one for us. Following retirement, Murray was able to stay by my side and help me through the upcoming months. Yes, it turned out to be a beautiful blessing. Thank you, Lord!

Eight days had passed since my last testing series in Birmingham, and I knew the results from the evaluations would arrive soon. Actually, before any official liver transplant placement can be made, all medical records must be examined and approved by the insurance provider. Two days later, I finally received the long overdue letter from UAB. The letter stated that I was a candidate for liver transplant. Oh, Lord, I was so grateful. Thank you, God! Had I not been accepted into the transplant program, I probably would not be alive today. People everywhere were so pleased and thankful when they learned the good news about the possible transplant. It was evident that many hearts had been touched during this time, including my own.

Before week's end, I would be packing again for my return to Birmingham. I had an appointment with Dr. Bynon to go over the next procedure before we could advance to the next level.

Despite the painful and upsetting past few months, I felt very fortunate to have had so many years of relatively good health since my diagnosis of primary biliary cirrhosis fifteen years earlier. When someone has primary biliary cirrhosis, the bile ducts are slowly destroyed, and I had reached the end stage of deterioration. The clock continued to click, and I remembered the comforting words of the disciple James, "At the heart of every storm is victory, just waiting to be claimed."

*Thought for today:*_____

"Give thanks to the Lord, for he is good! His faithful love endures forever" (Psalm 107: 1 NLT).

CHAPTER 5

A Shade of Orange

What a surprise! Murray's Uncle Bob and Aunt Pauline had stopped in from a trip from their home state of North Carolina. That was good medicine; they are two of the best people you could ever hope to meet. I knew they were shocked when they saw me that day. The energetic person they had always known was now much weaker and unable to stay up for very long. I could see their concern as they looked into my eyes, which incidentally had taken on a yellow pigment because of high bilirubin. Honestly, as I told them, I wished all of this had been a bad dream; however, to my disappointment, it was a reality. Nonetheless, I was so glad they had come. There was no end to all the wonderful things these two people did for us. In fact, they're responsible for a lot of what we have today. This trip was not any different because they brought me some good news. Their prayer committee at the church that they attended was not only praying for me but would also come to the church at the time of my surgery and pray continuously until it was over, regardless of the time or day. I could not imagine anyone doing this for me, let alone going in the middle of the night; but praise the Lord, they did just that.

It was really good seeing both Bob and Pauline, and they could not have picked a better time to come. When the time came for them to go on the road again, bidding farewell was very difficult.

There were so many details and responsibilities to address, especially after a very destructive hailstorm in our area, one that had destroyed not only our roof but also the liner in the pool and all our outdoor furniture. What a mess! On top of everything else, now we had to arrange to get everything repaired. Then again, I realized that what I was facing really made all of the storm damage seem minor by comparison.

I found it interesting to watch as the workers relined the pool, so I glued myself to a chair and looked at them working. After all, I was getting to the point that I hated to go out in public because many people could not help but stare at me nowadays. My yellow skin—or maybe I should say orange skin—made me look like a pumpkin. Positive thoughts were really what I needed; however, gloom and doom seemed to be knocking at the door again. I knew it was hard for everyone involved, not just for myself.

Jackie's situation was always a constant worry for all of us. We could see that the pregnancy had taken its toll on her. The baby's survival had been so important, but now Jackie herself was in grave danger. What could we do? There were just too many storms going on in our lives!

The following week, we prepared ourselves for yet another trip to UAB, where we would meet with Dr. Bynon and discuss a procedure that was definitely needed, one that another doctor would perform there at the clinic. Apparently, there could be no transplant unless they first performed this procedure. The liver tumor had reached its maximum growth and had to be treated with chemo immediately. I had to admit that this news really scared me, and I was beginning to wonder what would actually happen.

It was very late when we left the clinic that day, and I knew Murray's mother, Annie, better known as Maw-Maw, was anxiously awaiting our call along with everyone else. As usual, she was always worrying about me; however, I knew Murray's sister, Carolyn, would come soon and take good care of Maw-Maw. She, too, is another person who is very dear to my heart. Both Murray and I have sweet families. Oh, indeed, what precious memories we do have. I definitely found that you think about a lot of things when you're looking into the face of grave uncertainty.

When we arrived home that evening, we found that the workers had finished refurbishing the pool and replacing the roof. The previous storm had really played havoc in the entire area. We noticed that many people had property destroyed; it actually looked as if a tornado had ripped through the countryside. I had never dreamed that hail could be so destructive, but I learned that hail the size of baseballs would do a lot of property damage. Luckily, no one was injured. All the hammering and banging managed to keep my mind off of myself for the remainder of that week.

Oh, boy, the notes and cards were pouring in, but all the beautifully embroidered angels coming in from the Angel Ministry all around the United States were totally amazing. Each one was so special, and every single one came with a card and a prayer. I knew my dearest friend, Cherry Sue, was responsible for all of this, and I couldn't thank her enough because each one of those angels was so dear to my heart. I will treasure them always.

It is so wonderful to know that there are many people left in this world who truly care. These are the ones who really make a difference and set a good example for us all, especially when we know that it is not a duty to them but a genuine blessing from the heart.

I was unable to do very much in the next few days because I was declining rapidly. When I looked in the mirror, I would stare to see if my eyes looked worse than they had the day before. I knew that both my skin and eyes let everyone know that I certainly had a serious liver disease.

At the time, Jackie was no better either. In fact, she was much worse, so Charlie, her husband, tried to work and care for her as much as possible. There again, our hands were tied, and we were terribly afraid something might happen to her. She was in and out of the hospital every couple of weeks. Everything that could go wrong seemed to be happening. When Jackie first told us that they were expecting a baby, I was very concerned because she already had a serious bladder disease, and sure enough, the pregnancy made it worse. We were so thankful she had such a wonderful husband, one who had just recently served military duty in Iraq. Charlie had returned home and married Jackie, and then seven months later, they learned that they had a child on the way.

Murray and I had both grown mentally and physically tired, yet we knew the journey was far from over.

*Thought for today:*_____

"Therefore do not worry about tomorrow, for tomorrow will worry about itself. Each day has enough trouble of its own" (Matthew 6:34 NIV).

CHAPTER 6

Vascular Data

Easter was over, and my parents left for their home in Eustis, Florida. Before they left, they came by to say their goodbyes. As always, it was a good visit; however, I realized that Mom and Dad were deeply worried about my condition. No parent wants to think that losing a child is a possibility. Our conversation went on for several hours, and like all good things, it came to an end. At that moment, I wondered, *How am I going to tell them both goodbye?* This was indeed an awful moment, but we managed with many tears. Although I went to bed totally depressed, I made myself read for a little while. Reading always seemed to calm my nerves, and after I looked through many books, I chose the Bible as I often do. There is a lot to be learned from the Scriptures, not to mention the comfort found in their readings. One of my very favorites was Psalm 91. This was and is an excellent chapter for anyone who faces many fears. In fact, I found myself reading this chapter daily and still do.

Many mornings, I awakened to the sun slowly rising. I never

knew how to appreciate the magnificent beauty of every sunrise and sunset until I became ill. It was then that I realized how we get so caught up in our daily lives that we sometimes forget how truly blessed we really are. Another blessing for me was all the beautiful weather we had each time we went to Birmingham. There was always that fear of a storm brewing while en route to the hospital, but thankfully, that didn't happen. There again, looking for the worst was just my nature. So instead of thinking negative thoughts, I tried to always remember the Bible verse found in Philippians 4:13: "I can do all things through Christ which strengtheneth me." This was the one verse that I repeated most often, and as a result, I learned how to appreciate many things during those trials.

That following day, we travelled to Birmingham, and as usual, the journey was long and tiring. The vascular clinic, where the TACE procedure was performed, was located in a different area than the liver department, which was a little easier to access. After we reached the waiting area, we could see that it was quite large, which made it easier to accommodate many people who came for the procedure. Thankfully, Jeanie had gone with us, and both she and Murray were allowed to go to the back with me. After I signed in and answered many questions, I was sent to a small room with a bed. I was so cold and terribly nervous, but a nurse came to my rescue with some warming blankets that felt absolutely heavenly. A few minutes later, a technician arrived to talk with the three of us. The discussion lasted a good two hours. Needless to say, we were all tired. There was a lot of material to go over, so it was late afternoon before we were able to leave.

The following information is some of the data I received

regarding the procedure: TACE (transarterial chemoembolization) is a treatment for liver cancer. Chemotherapy is injected into the hepatic (liver) artery that supplies the tumor with material. TACE can shrink the tumor, which can give a person the option for surgery. Otherwise, I would not be eligible because of my tumor's size. We expected an overnight stay in the hospital for observation purposes. I had to admit that by the time I heard all the facts and the risk factors, I was horrified. Oh my! I expected that nothing about the procedure was going to be simple. Within minutes, Dr. Saddekni, the specialist, had come in to meet me. The moment I met him, I knew without a doubt that I was in good hands. There was just something about him that made me feel at ease. I had felt that same peaceful feeling when I had met Dr. Bynon. Everyone at the clinic had been so kind and informative. I started praying from that moment on that the procedure scheduled two weeks from that day would be successful.

After we returned home, I found myself gathering even more information about the TACE procedure. There was definitely a lot of information to be found online, and what I had read was not very encouraging. I had hoped for better results than the ones I'd been reading.

The next week went by quickly, with friends dropping in to visit while others came to sit for the day. I liked that, especially because I hated being alone. Murray could take a much needed break .There was one particular friend of mine, Cherry Sue, who not only came when needed but was there even when she wasn't well herself. We had the best conversations about everything. In fact, we both dropped off to sleep while we were talking. She, too, had so many health issues, and yet nothing stood in the way of her coming. Her encouraging words really touched my heart. Cherry Sue was and still is a great friend today.

There had been a lot of time to sit and think of all my friends and loved ones while I was ill, but what really stands out in my mind is how Jeanie was there for me constantly. I knew we loved each other, but I never realized how much. We argued a lot of times, as sisters do, but she always knew that our disagreements would pass. Then there was Murray, who was always there for me, and at night when my fears were at their worst, I'd hold on to him tightly. What would I have done without these two? No, not two, but three, because Johnny definitely was there too.

It was a little past noon when the pastor from Beulah, a small neighboring church, was knocking at the front door. I had attended that church as a small child, I remembered, and it held many memories for me. Brother Tim Bass, who was the pastor there, knew of my sickness and came to visit. His presence was a blessing because I had known Tim and his family for many years. He's a genuine man who loves and cares for all the people. In the South, we call preachers like Tim "God-called preachers." That visit was the first of many more to come, and each week thereafter, he was there for me and my family.

After I sat for several hours one day, I realized that my side was beginning to cramp once again, and my feet were twice their normal size. There was nothing I could do or take other than Tylenol. How depressing all this was, but I knew that God was with me and would see me through this ordeal. For some strange reason, though, I had to keep reassuring myself. "Why?" I asked, but then again, I knew that this feeling was just the old gloom and doom creeping back in—or should I say "the Devil himself?"

*Thought for today:*_____

"The Lord himself goes before you and will be with you; he will never leave you nor forsake you" (Deuteronomy 31:8 NLT).

CHAPTER 7

Us Four and No More!

Many cards with sweet notes were coming in the mail daily, and I loved them all. Everyone in the church and the community had been so dedicated to keeping in touch. I was also receiving a lot of literature relating to transplants, including the procedure for the transplant itself. The advancements in today's medical technology and practices are amazing.

I had begun questioning the possibility and probability of locating a liver that would be a compatible match for me. With so many people already on the list, I could not imagine the transplant surgery in the immediate future. In addition, my MELD score was elevated, which made the shrinkage of the tumor a frightening uncertainty. My mind was full of questions and fears. I knew nothing about transplants or any kind of surgery with the exception of a hysterectomy. That was major enough, and now I would have a *liver transplant!* Every day became a challenge, and at times, I didn't choose to accept the reality of everything that was turning my world upside down.

The fear of dying haunted me every waking moment. I was definitely afraid to die. That's where Johnny really helped me understand my fears and made sure I understood the plan of salvation. And although I did understand and was fully committed to God, I was still afraid. Thereafter, Jeanie and Johnny made it a point to talk with me each night, and before they left for the evening, Johnny would hold my hand and pray the most beautiful prayers. They always left me with such a peaceful feeling. This went on night after night, and as I look back, I realize that God was not only dealing with me but also touching the hearts of everyone involved.

Many family members, Brother Tim Bass, and friends called to reassure us that they would be at the hospital for the TACE procedure. That news was a great comfort to me. I knew that being there would not be necessary for everyone and that it was really quite a distance for some to travel; however, I was also very pleased because I knew they would be there in person and would be praying for me, and that was what I needed most—prayer.

Many times when I listen to people pray, I think about my mom and dad. They had always been such good prayer warriors, and my dad … well, he can pray the most meaningful prayers and still does to this day. Then there is Mom, who I honestly believe has a direct line to heaven. If you walked into a room where she had been praying, believe me, you would know it: The room is aglow, and we have all witnessed this phenomenon.

When I was growing up, we never showed a lot of emotions in our family. Instead, we usually kept everything pretty much to ourselves. However, we have certainly made up for that lately as the tears have really flowed. Although Mom and Dad are now up in their years, Jeanie and I both know that we are still little girls in their eyes and always will be. We've been so fortunate to have them both in this life, and hopefully, they will have many years yet to come. As children, our dad always said, "Us four and no more!" Of course, our family increased over the years, and they love them all. I just hated that my illness was weighing so heavily on their minds, yet I was also thankful for them and all their prayers.

With all those thoughts behind me, I began to have other concerns regarding the TACE procedure. I knew I had never been put to sleep with general anesthesia, so naturally, I thought, *How would I be put to sleep?* The thought scared me. I guess I had seen too many medical procedures on television. Years ago when I had undergone a hysterectomy, I chose to have a spinal, and that was it. I hated the thought of being tubed.

Later that week, Jackie called and insisted on coming to see me. This adamant request really concerned us because we knew she was not able to travel. Doctors had begun to express their doubts about the baby making it to full term because Jackie already had many things wrong with her. She suffered from interstitial cystitis, a bladder disease, along with eclampsia and high blood pressure. So much was happening at one time. To our open arms and hearts, she arrived looking tired but very pretty. We talked about many things but mostly about our feelings for one another and how the Lord would see us both through this difficult time in both our lives. Our conversation was good and gave us both a peace of mind.

My energy level had gotten quite low, so I rested most of the time. The indigestion was continuous, and my ribcage ached constantly. A good heating pad stayed with me at all times. My legs looked awful and were twice their normal size, splotchy, and red in color. My arms were easily bruised and littered with purple patches caused by bleeding under the skin. My hair was beginning to thin, and my skin was quite dry. I could see all the changes that had been developing over a long period of time. Apparently, others were seeing the same thing. Although I covered the illness up in the best way I could, the yellow eyes were there to stay.

The following day, I finished packing for the one-night hospital stay. There were many things to attend to before I left, but I knew Murray would take care of everything. He had already endured so much with me, and yet this new phase of the journey had only begun. Most people have no idea of the constant and trying demands of being a caregiver until they've walked in the shoes of a caregiver for months on end. You just pray that these loving people can hang in there because those are the ones on whom you have become so dependent. There must certainly be a special reward in heaven for caregivers after they serve as God's chosen helpers on earth.

*Thought for today:*_____

"He will cover you with his feathers. He will shelter you with his wings. His faithful promises are your armor and protection. Do not be afraid of the terrors of the night, nor the arrow that flies in the day. Do not dread the disease that stalks in darkness, nor the disaster that strikes at midday" (Psalm 91:4–6 NLT).

CHAPTER 8

Job Well Done

There's no doubt about it. The day had been an especially long one. After we talked extensively about the TACE procedure, it suddenly became a reality. At first, I was a little apprehensive about being put to sleep. I guess that was normal, especially when there was so much uncertainty involved.

Pastor Tim Bass called and said he planned to be at the hospital by the time we arrived. Just knowing he would be there made me feel a lot better. Well, it looked as if we were ready to go. I mentioned to Jeanie how I had talked to Mom and Dad the night before and how they had told me that they would be praying all day. I really needed to hear that because they were such good prayer warriors. Everyone else knew we were leaving, and as much as I hated to go, we left.

It was early in the day when we arrived at the clinic but not long before a nurse had called me back. After I changed into a lovely regulation hospital gown, the nurses began to let different people in to visit. To my surprise, fourteen members of my family had come to be with us, which really made me feel a whole lot better. It was comforting to know that the pastor was there because he made sure everyone in the waiting room stayed calm. I knew that most people could feel on edge when they were just sitting around. The nurse let two at a time come in for a visit. It was good seeing everyone and all our children. I knew most of them had travelled a long way, and what a surprise it was to see Jackie and Charlie. I could tell she was in a lot of pain. Hopefully, the trip had not been too hard on her. How wonderful it would have been if I could have turned all this around and could have been there for her. I knew that was just wishful thinking.

The nurse came to start the IV and reminded us that it might be thirty or forty minutes longer before the staff took me to surgery. While we were waiting, Pastor Tim gathered all of my family, and together, they prayed for me. This was definitely a scary moment, but I knew I was in good hands. Slowly but surely, my journey proceeded forward. The nurses wheeled me into a large operating room, and many different members of the surgical team surrounded me. I remember feeling a little woozy, but what I remember most was everyone rushing around like the little elves at Santa's workshop. One by one, I asked who they were and what they were doing. None of them gave replies, just smiles. At that moment, I'm sure I sounded a little goofy. Then out of nowhere, they brought a mask down and placed it over my nose. I definitely started to panic until I realized that the man standing next to me was Dr. Saddekni himself. I remember his gentle smile and immediately felt at ease. That was it then. I was *out!* The next thing I heard was a voice saying, "Mrs. Knox, you've been asleep for quite some time."

I couldn't believe it was over—or at least that part of it was. Thirty minutes later, I was leaving recovery. To my surprise, there was my cheering squad, all fourteen of them. I remember asking for Tim Bass (pastor) to pray for me, which he did. Afterwards, one by one, they began to leave; however, they weren't headed for home. No, they were going out for lunch. Apparently, Jeanie was the only one left in the waiting room then. Naturally, everyone else thought it would be a while before we knew anything. Well, to Jeanie's surprise, Dr. Saddekni came out to report, "Everything went beautiful." This was indeed a miracle because the doctors had been questioning if the tumor had been completely surrounded with chemo. Thank you, Lord.

Everyone was delighted over the good news, and before I knew it, I was on my way to the eighth floor. While I was transferred, Murray received a call from my coordinator, Peggy Cochran, stating that all had been cleared for my transplant. I had been placed second on the waiting list.

We were both so excited over the news, although I was still a bit incoherent from the drugs, nothing really registering at that moment. One thing I did remember, though, was that I was back on the original floor I had been on earlier—the transplant floor.

Several hours passed, and my mind was a little clearer when I learned that an Angio-Seal had been placed in my upper thigh. Instead of using a sandbag, the doctors used this vascular closure device, and my body would adapt to its presence within ninety days. Therefore, I would need to be careful during this time because that was the place where the doctors had entered the artery. Ouch!

Overall, I would say things went great. My only thought

was that the procedure proved to be successful. Murray stayed that night, and Jody, our youngest son, remained with us till late evening. All my family had been there that day. Oh, how I do appreciate them all.

Although I slept rather well that night, when morning came, I still felt relatively tired. Good news arrived a little after breakfast when Dr. Eckhoff came in to say that we could go home .Yeah! That was music to our ears. After we signed all the necessary papers, we had some lunch before we checked out.

Still not feeling too well, I had barely gotten out of Birmingham when my side started hurting. I thought the riding might be causing some discomfort, but as time went on, I realized the pain wasn't just from being in the car. My side was getting worse, and I couldn't stay still. Gas pressure was building rapidly under my ribcage. The pain had gotten to the point where Murray had to stop and pull off the roadway. I could barely move, and sitting had become unbearable. We finally pulled over at a gas station that was close to home so that I could get out and stretch my legs. Hopefully, that would relieve some of the pressure, I thought. Murray walked me nonstop back and forth for what seemed like an hour. we actually left later in the day, but thankfully, we made it home with no further complications. I went straight to bed, my mind flooded with fears. It was obvious that my condition had gotten worse.

Jeanie was working that day, but Murray managed to get in touch with her. Later that evening, both Jeanie and Johnny came by the house, and what she found was unexpected. I was crying out in pain, unable to sit still. The gas was building under my ribcage all around my liver. I didn't know what was happening, but I did know I couldn't endure the pain much longer. Immediately, Jeanie got me out of the bed and made me start walking. We walked back and forth from one end of the house to the other for over an hour. All I could do was hold on to her shoulders when I suddenly caught a glimpse of the two of us in a long mirror. Although the pain was excruciating, I couldn't help but smile. We looked like the Little Engine that Could climbing up the hill, declaring, "I think I can. I think I can."

Even though the gas eased from the walking, the pain remained severe. I told Jeanie I wouldn't be able to tolerate the agony for very long, and if this was the way it was going to be, God needed to take me on. The pain was so intense. Jeanie realized my agony and helped me get back in bed. I was so afraid of her leaving me, but I did manage to calm down after taking some sleeping medication that caused me to drift off. Murray never left my side that evening.

The next morning, I felt somewhat better, but I still suffered a lot of pain radiating from the tumor. Shortly after I got up, Jeanie called from work, and I could detect the concern in her voice. She wanted me to know that everyone had been updated on my condition and that all would be praying. That was great for me because I knew prayers by the multitudes meant that even more prayers were going up . Murray was with me the rest of that day, along with Jeanie and Johnny, who came that evening.

Thought for today:_____

"Weeping may remain for a night, but rejoicing
comes in the morning" (Psalm 30:5 KJV).

CHAPTER 9

Unexpected Call

Several weeks had passed since the TACE procedure, and believe it or not, I was actually beginning to feel somewhat better. It never crossed my mind that the chemotherapy might be shrinking the tumor, but thankfully, it did. By the time we went back to Birmingham, the tumor had shrunk from 5.0 to 4.5cm in measurement. Another blessing! Thank you, Lord, for your unfailing goodness and mercy.

One thing was for sure: We had a bountiful supply of food on our table at all times. My cousin Rita along with the church members and community friends didn't stop bringing entire meals, including decadent desserts. It was so overwhelming to see how many people actually cared and wanted to help.

When the month of April arrived, I knew that Jeanie and Johnny would be anxiously waiting to leave for their home in Montana. This was the time of year that they closed up their house in Alabama and headed for high country. My heart ached because I knew I would be lost without Jeanie, but I understood.

Previously, the hospital staff had told me that they could call me at any time since I had become second on the waiting list for a liver transplant. Jeanie had decided to postpone their Montana move until June if necessary, and I was hoping to have my surgery by that time. My thoughts were racing. Would we really find a liver, and if so, would it come before June? I didn't know for sure, but I did realize it had to come in God's own timing and not when everyone else, including me, wanted it. We would all just have to keep the faith and be patient and wait.

The sun rose, and the sun set, and with each passing day, I started feeling much better than earlier weeks. As I was growing stronger, the spring temperatures were also improving, making it possible for Murray and me to take daily strolls to help build my strength and relieve stress. Anything I could do would certainly work in my favor.

Another week passed, and a new one started. The weather was beautiful, nothing out of the ordinary, just pleasant days and sunny skies. This particular day, Murray and I were just sitting around and listening to the news when the phone rang. It was Robbie Jones, Murray's first cousin from North Carolina. I immediately thought he was calling to check on me, and because he was Uncle Bob's son, I knew he was aware of my condition. I was wrong, wrong, wrong! Robbie had called to say that his sister-in-law had just passed away and that because she had been a donor, he and his wife, Kay, who was sister to the donor, had requested her liver for me. Needless to say, we were *shocked!* I listened as Murray continued to talk. It was true. They wanted me to have her liver. Murray immediately got busy working on his long list of phone calls. He placed one call to the hospital in North Carolina and another to my doctor at UAB. Everything was happening so quickly that I became dizzy, and I wondered, *Will this really work?* Her blood type had to be compatible with mine, and at that time, we didn't even know what her blood type was. After he received all the information from Robbie, Murray started the calls, which kept him busy for hours on end. Then the call we were looking for came. Dr. Bynon's office at UAB confirmed that her blood type was definitely a match. She was a universal donor, type O. This was absolutely wonderful news, although we needed more coordinating calls between both hospitals before we received the final okay to come to Birmingham.

I was about as numb as a human could get, and I wondered if I was hearing everything correctly. If so, then this would be an absolute miracle. Who would have ever thought something like this could happen, especially because this was Robbie's wife's sister, a relative of a relative. Her death was terrible news for all of them, yet they had thought of me. Without a shadow of doubt, I knew that God was truly in control.

Around 1:00 a.m., we received the phone call from UAB. They were ready for me to come in. I knew the moment I heard the phone ring that I was about to begin yet another important phase of my journey—the *transplant* itself.

*Thought for today:*_____

"You thrill me, Lord, with all you have done for me! I sing for joy because of what you have done" (Psalm 92:4–5 NLT).

47

CHAPTER 10

Ready! Set! Go!

Murray continued contacting family and friends, and the news about my imminent transplant surgery quickly spread everywhere.

Around 2:00 a.m., Jeanie arrived at our house, but a funny scene actually transpired in the next few moments. Murray and Jeanie were scurrying around like little ground squirrels while I waited patiently in the car. It was hard to say who was more nervous—Jeanie or Murray. Silence filled the air as we headed north to Birmingham. It was as if each of us was deeply submerged in anxious anticipation of the next few hours, submerged in earnest prayer for God's blessing and in total fear as well. Every town we passed was like a ghost town, completely silent. Just the overwhelming news of the transplant had left us speechless as well.

The long two-hour drive seemed more like four before we nervously arrived at UAB. What luck, we actually found a parking place right at the entry door. However, there was no getting around the extensive processing procedure, which seemed to take forever. I was then taken by wheelchair to the eighth floor, which was the transplant floor. It's hard to explain what I was actually feeling at that moment; however, I do remember being scared half to death. My heart was pounding as we reached an empty hospital room. Shortly thereafter, the nurses sent everyone to a small waiting area, and my prep work began, starting with a shower using an antibacterial solution. While I was in there alone, I remember asking myself, "Is this really all happening? Oh, Lord, it is just too much for me to take in. In fact, it is like a bad dream just waiting to happen."

It was much later before I was allowed to join my family in the hospital room, where we somewhat patiently waited for yet another hour before the nurse arrived and took me to what I think they called the holding room. There, they drew some of my blood for testing and set up an IV. No one was allowed to see me for quite some time, and I remained in the holding area for several hours, which actually felt like several days. It was there in the holding room that a middle-age man who worked with anesthesia came by and talked with me. I can't remember his name, but he definitely saw the fear in my eyes. Once he learned about the nature of my illness, he assured me that I would be in excellent hands and that I shouldn't be afraid. His words were not only comforting but also accurate because I knew that was true with certainty. After all, I did have the Lord in one hand and Dr. Bynon in the other. That was good enough for me!

All the waiting was not easy. The uncertainty of not knowing if I would even survive such an intricate transplant surgery was hard on everyone. Everyone kept reassuring me that all would be fine, but I knew deep down that the outcome was up to the good Lord.

Several hours later, the staff finally allowed my family in the holding room. My children—Scottie along with his wife, Mary Jewell, Jody with his wife, Becky, Jeanie, and my dear, sweet husband, Murray—everyone was there except Jackie and Charlie. My little girl was too sick to come, and my heart ached for her terribly. Between the surgery and her absence, I literally felt sick. It was then that I asked both my boys to promise me that they would keep an eye on Jackie and Charlie. Murray was the last one I spoke to before I went into the surgical area. We were like most couples who had their share of ups and downs through the years, but overall, everything had been pretty good. We had been married for over forty years, and hopefully, we would see our seventieth wedding anniversary as my parents had recently enjoyed.

The moment had come. I knew the team was ready for me when I saw the nurses dressed in surgical attire. It was time for me to go. Murray leaned over to kiss me goodbye and said he would see me later. No doubt about it, he had all the confidence and faith in the world that I was going to return. As the stretcher began to roll, I could see the surgical team behind a partial glass wall. It was real. They were waiting for me! They were ready for me! After all, I had been waiting for months, praying for God's intervention, and finally, it was time; however, I still didn't feel quite ready yet. Then suddenly, without warning, I remembered no more.

*Thought for today:*_____

"Even though I walk through the valley of the shadow of death, I will fear no evil, for you are with me; your rod and your staff, they comfort me" (Psalm 23:4 KJV).

CHAPTER 11

The Grand Finale

The surgery that had haunted me for so many years was about to begin. The staff led my family to a waiting room where a large screen displayed the progress of each surgical patient, enabling them to track the progress of patients.

Two hours after I was taken by the surgical team, several misadventures started developing. My grandson, Justin, who is always thinking of others, was downstairs giving blood. Although his blood was a match with mine, he passed out before he completed the donation, and his mom helped revive him with splashes of water in his face. Another complication was unfolding upstairs as well. To everyone's amazement, the name P. Knox started flashing on the progress board, indicating that P. Knox was in recovery and was doing well. Two hours? That was really fast surgery! Friends and family were in shock yet pleased with the information, so some left to return to their homes and workplaces because the doctors would not allow visitors for at least a couple of days.

Murray, however, was still in shock as he made his way to the nurses' station to get more details about my condition. Needless to say, he was stunned once again when that nurse told him that my surgery had not yet begun. "What!" he replied. "How can that be when my wife's name is on the screen showing that she is in recovery?" The nurse looked up and could not believe what she was seeing. When she realized that someone had probably made a terrible mistake, she started investigating and learned that there were two patients with the name P. Knox. It was the other P. Knox whose surgery was completed, not mine. Who would have ever thought in a million years that this could happen? What a mess! Phone calls immediately went out to visitors who had already left.

In the midst of the mad confusion, Dr. Bynon sent out his head nurse to see what was going on and to explain that my surgery was just about to begin. Actually, the helicopter at that time was landing with my donor's liver, and the medical professionals would then deliver it directly to surgery. Talk about an unusual mix-up! Two patients going by P. Knox in a large hospital both having surgery the same day? Very strange.

Within the hour, the surgery began, and after five long hours, Dr. Bynon came out to the waiting area to discuss the transplant procedure and my progress. He apologized for the earlier mix-up and said, "I may be fast but not that fast, and so far, a two-hour transplant has never been done."

My family prayed and received many words of encouragement in the waiting room that day. A wonderful lady even sent me a beautiful cross that had been blessed by prayer. I don't know who all of these people were, and my family doesn't either; however, I do know that people like that woman are a blessing and are dearly appreciated. The prayer cross is a reminder to me of answered prayers, and the cross still rests on my nightstand right next to my head.

I had completed a major phase in my journey, but I was just starting the major challenge, the recovery phase. The next forty-eight hours following surgery were crucial, so I was taken to the surgical intensive-care unit, where I was carefully monitored for the following two days. In ICU, I remained on a respirator for a short time, and although I moaned for no apparent reason, my family was frequently reassured that I was doing well. Thank you, Lord.

The third day following surgery, I was taken to a private room on the eighth floor. Boy, was I tipsy. I could not seem to focus on anything, but I do remember Jeanie staying with me that night. It was actually the fourth day when the reality of the surgery began to set in. Naturally, the first thing I wanted to see was my stomach. Wow! The doctors had literally sawed me in half. It looked like I had a hundred staples, and I probably did. My abdomen had been opened with an incision that looked like an upside-down "Y" that began at the breastbone and extended down along the ribs on both sides. There were also three oblong drains that the surgeons had placed around the liver before they had closed my abdomen. I called those my little chamber pots, but they actually resembled small hand grenades and proved to be quite a nuisance. My pain from the surgery was not that bad, but my back was killing me, probably from lying on a steel table for so many hours. I vaguely remember acting weird, and most of the time, my conversations were pretty crazy. I later learned that I was on 500mg of prednisone. No wonder I didn't make any sense. Apparently, my liver had been in transport for a long period of time, and my body was trying to reject it. The next day, Dr. Dubay, another transplant surgeon, told us that my liver enzymes were beginning to stabilize. Dr. Dubay was an excellent doctor I saw quite a lot of while I remained in the hospital. What a group! These three were some of the best transplant surgeons a person could hope for.

I guess one of the hardest things for me was trying to walk. I couldn't seem to make my feet move in the direction I wanted to walk. That was definitely a strange feeling. Therapy was what I needed, and that's what I got several times a day. My energy level seemed to be nonexistent, and no matter how hard I tried to walk, I was utterly exhausted. That was something that I had to really work on and still do to this day.

The nursing staff was fantastic, and when it came to rock 'n' roll, they rolled. They were on the move constantly. Now that's what I call a nursing staff. Thank you, Beverly and all the nurses on the liver transplant wing. With my craziness, I probably strained their patience, so they probably thought of me as a little less than wonderful, but regardless, I am thankful for them all.

During my hospital stay, I saw different members of the team as well as the nurses. There was Peggy, my liver transplant coordinator; the physical therapist; the dietician; the pharmacist; and others that educated me about my liver transplant. There was still another team member that showed me how to give myself insulin shots while I was taking prednisone. I caught on quickly, so that didn't prove to be a problem, and as the doctors decreased the prednisone, my sugar levels decreased as well. By week's end, they removed the IV that I had been wearing in my jugular vein, and although I was dreading its removal, the process wasn't that bad. Next, they needed to remove the three drains—or chamber pots, as I might say. That was no picnic, as one by one, they painfully came out. Ouch!

My balance seemed to improve with every step despite the medication, which kept me partially confused and emotionally disoriented. But what the heck! I was thankful to be alive! I was hospitalized for one week, and then the transplant wing released me to the UAB Townhouse, where my convalescence would continue.

Amazingly, what was supposed to be a six-week stay turned out to only last for one week. Yes, I was making small steps toward a beautiful recovery. Thank you, Lord, and thank you, Dr. Bynon. I also want to thank Dr. Eckhoff and Dr. Dubay, too. All three of them were and still are a blessing to mankind to this day.

*Thought for today:*_____

"Oh give thanks to the Lord, for He is good; for His loving kindness is everlasting" (1 Chronicles 16:34 NASB).

Epilogue

I have enjoyed many sunrises and sunsets since my liver transplant, and overall, I am doing quite well. When we were pulling out of our drive and heading toward UAB for my surgery, I remember looking back and wondering if that might be my last trip, my last glimpse of life as I knew it, an existence I loved.

The surgery was a success. I did return home, and I began my lengthy convalescence. Every day became a little easier for me, and I was soon able to walk more. And after a brief period of time, I was able to take short excursions. My wise dad always advised, "It's a cinch by the inch but hard by the yard." And that is just what I did. I "inched" my way to better health.

My energy level is not where it once was, but it is slowly improving with proper exercise and health care. Every six months, I return to UAB for a CAT scan, and every two months, I go for lab work to monitor and maintain

"Thank You Lord I made it"

my progress. Deep within my abdomen, I can still feel the end of a stitch remaining from the transplant surgery. Dr. Bynon says it's his signature, but for me, it's my constant reminder that God gave me a second chance at life like Dorcas from the Bible.

The Ultimate Gift

My transplant was an emotional and physical journey that I had to go through alone, but praise the Lord that a donor's organ became available for me. The woman I received the organ from not only saved my life but also several others.

I've read on the internet under organ donations that more than eighteen people die every day in the United States while they are waiting for organs. What most people don't realize is that up to eight lives can be saved by one donor and that the same donor can improve the lives of up to fifty people by donating their tissues and corneas. Wow! I find that amazing. One person can do all this, yet so many people will never receive the organs that they desperately need. There are just not enough donors. It's sad but true.

Only you have the power to save lives. Giving an organ is the most precious gift that you could ever leave behind whether a family member or a complete stranger receives your donation. I know because I received that ultimate gift and realized that God still has a purpose for me.

Phillis & Murray
Author & husband

Scottie & Mary-Jewell Knox
Son and Daughter n law

Jennifer & Brady Knox
(Grand-children)

Upper right-Jody-(son & family)
Center-Justin
Left-Becky
Lower R.. Jessie

Jackie &Charlie Browder
daughter & husband

Isabella Browder
(Grand-daughter) and Miracle Child

Glenn E. Browder
(grand-son)

Philip & Ollie Earnest (Mom and Dad)

Jeanie & Johnny Turner
(Sister and husband)

Carolyn Mitchell
(sister n law)
Annie Knox
(Maw-Maw)